𝔐𝔢𝔡𝔦𝔠𝔞𝔩 𝔒𝔣𝔣𝔦𝔠𝔢𝔯𝔰 𝔬𝔣 𝔖𝔠𝔥𝔬𝔬𝔩𝔰 𝔄𝔰𝔰𝔬𝔠𝔦𝔞𝔱𝔦𝔬𝔫.

THE

MANAGEMENT OF ATHLETICS

IN

PUBLIC SCHOOLS

A PAPER READ BEFORE THE ASSOCIATION
On January 12th, 1886.

BY

GEORGE FLETCHER, M.D. Cantab.
of Highgate

LATE MEDICAL OFFICER OF ALBERT COLLEGE, FRAMLINGHAM AND SCHOLAR OF
CLARE COLLEGE, CAMBRIDGE

Printed by Order of the Association

LONDON
H. K. LEWIS, 136 GOWER STREET, W.C.
1886

MEDICAL OFFICERS OF SCHOOLS ASSOCIATION.

President.

THOMAS FULLER, M.D., M.R.C.S., Medical Officer, St. Nicholas College, Lancing.

Vice-President.

SURGEON-MAJOR EVATT, M.D., L.R.C.S.I., A.M.S., Medical Officer, Royal Military Academy, Woolwich.

Treasurer.

NOBLE SMITH, L.R.C.P., F.R.C.S.E., Surgeon, All Saints Children's Hospital, London.

Honorary Secretaries.

ALDER SMITH, M.B., F.R.C.S., Medical Officer, Christ's Hospital, London.
CHARLES E. SHELLY, B.A., M.B., M.R.C.S., Medical Officer, Haileybury College.

Members of Council.

FLETCHER BEACH, M.B., M.R.C.P., Medical Superintendent, Darenth Asylum, Dartford.

ALFRED BRETT, M.D., M.R.C.S., Medical Officer, London Orphan Asylum, Watford.

GEORGE BRIGGS, M.B, M.R.C.S., one of the Medical Officers, Harrow School.

BRIGADE-SURGEON CLARKE, M.D, M.R.C.S., A.M.S., Medical Officer, Royal Military College, Sandhurst.

ADAMS CLARKE, L.K.Q.C.P., L.R.C.S.I., Medical Officer, St. Pancras Industrial Schools, Leavesden.

ROBERT FARQUHARSON, M.P., LL.D., M.D., F.R C.P., formerly Medical Officer, Rugby School.

GEORGE FLETCHER, M.A., M.D., M.R.C.S., Highgate, formerly Medical Officer, Albert Memorial College, Framlingham.

C. W. HAIG-BROWN, M.D., C.M., M.R.C.S., Medical Officer, Charterhouse, Godalming.

O'BRIEN JONES, F.R.C.S, L.S.A., Medical Officer, Epsom College.

SURGEON-MAJOR LEVER, M.B, M.R.C.S., A.M.S., Medical Officer, Military College, Oxford.

H. JOHN PRANGLEY, L.R.C.P., M.R.C.S., Medical Officer, North Surrey District Schools, Anerley.

HUGH STATHAM, M.R.C.S., L.S.A., Medical Officer, Foundling Hospital, London.

THE MANAGEMENT OF ATHLETICS

IN

PUBLIC SCHOOLS.

Mr. President and Gentlemen,

The selection of an appropriate and fitting TITLE to my paper has been a matter of some difficulty, for while I was desirous to discuss with you the whole system of Athletics in our Public Schools, yet it was scarcely my wish to enter into every branch of sport, nor to lay down hard and fast rules for ourselves as medical men, as regards clothes, training, hours for games, diet, etc., which could not be carried out. Rather, my paper was undertaken with the view of finding out the different methods of employing THE HOURS OF RECREATION at our various Public Schools; of finding out to what degree our different schools *encourage* healthy games, and what steps they take towards getting the boys to enter into those games, and whether they make games more or less compulsory for every *healthy* lad; then comparing the information so collected, to offer you some hints as to the best plans of managing hours of recreation, and seeing if by means of the doctor to the school, we cannot avert some of the evils athletics are SUPPOSED to bring about, and so train up a more healthy frame in the boy. One chief practical lesson to be kept in mind in connection with muscular exercise and athletics of every kind, is that abundant and varied exercise is necessary to encourage a health brain-growth, and if we recognize the truth of the old Latin motto, *Mens sana in corpore sano*, we shall give the masters more fruitful soil in which to sow

1

their seed, and they will not then grudge listening to the advice we COLLECTIVELY can offer them.

The true aim of school training is the due and harmonious development of all the faculties in our nature, not only the mental and spiritual, but also the physical and moral.

Such development depends upon many influences, amongst others upon the influence a boy's surroundings at school has upon him, and I believe those surroundings to be far more conducive to health and manly vigour at a public school than at home, where the customs of society often demand that the growing boys shall lead unwholesome and enervating lives, and I am sure that if the body suffers from neglect of healthy laws then the mind and morals often suffer with it, though there is no doubt that lately many enervating evil customs have been expelled from families owing to the healthy habits brought from our schools.

We shall find that athletic exercises have always been in favour with nations distinguished by military success, and so far as robust health and bodily vigour are concerned, the means taken for strengthening the frame for success in games at school, will generally be found to answer the end for turning out a more vigorous healthy man for fighting the battles of life.

We shall all agree that a large amount of exercise in pure air is required to keep growing lads in bodily health and vigour. This exercise ought to be of a kind to ensure the perfect development of every muscle and organ of the body, and also to call into active play the mental faculties, and to exhilarate the animal spirits. Much has been done of late years to improve the health and power of boys by better drainage and ventilation of our school-buildings, but still more remains to be done, and I trust we can lay some of the foundation stones in improving *by athletics* those habits which impart quicker circulation to the blood, health to the system, and at the same time elasticity to the mind.

By athletics I do not want you to understand that I mean simply the gymnasium, and the wonderful sights which can be seen there, nor Athletic Sports, a good specimen of which takes place yearly at Lillie Bridge between the two Universities. I mean every branch of athletic exercise which can improve the bodily health and vigour of a lad, in fact, the active use of limb and muscle in the open air, the sure sign of vitality more or less seen in every lad, and if duly trained is an essential element of national greatness; but mind that it is fairly trained, do not depress it by allowing too much cramwork in the schools, till our boys are walking encyclopœdias and feeble precocities, do not encourage cramming schools where proper exercise is impossible.

On the other hand, often the healthy exercises are regarded as an amusement, too little as a means of training mind as well as body. The proficiency of the few has been considered more than the advantage of the mass boy-community, and the fashion and extravagance of the present day, have extended their pestilential patronage to our athletes in various objectionable forms.

Physical education certainly requires to be almost as scientifically studied as *intellectual* education. We can scarcely expect head-masters with their present burdens to add yet a fresh load, but we know that if we as medical men lend a little more time to the study of these matters, then the head-masters will listen often gladly to any suggestions.

All agree in the abstract that the arrangements of school-life should be in accordance with known physiological laws; by this I mean the diet, the hours of meals, the temperature and ventilation of rooms, the intervals between meals and work, the length of school hours, and the maximum and minimum amount of daily exercise, the dress worn especially during exercise, the nature of the games encouraged, all these should be matters not of tradition or custom, but of careful and honourable subordination to health requirements. Now I for my part believe where evils of athletics are prominent, these things are not being carried out.

The physical training at MOST schools is undoubtedly good, but I fancy it is due to the SYSTEM of games enforced, partly by public opinion and tradition, and partly by the boy authorities in the school.

1—2

Let us see as far as possible that their physical training and health are not quite treated as secondary matters, by absurd hours for lessons, roll-call breaking up games, and that cruel and ignorant custom of depriving boys of their well-earned exercise by impositions and detentions. This in excess is as monstrous as to deprive a boy of sufficient food or sleep, and no objections which have been brought against corporal punishment, appear to take into account the evils of impositions written during a considerable part of out-door play hours.

This step, however, may be the fault of the British public having raised such an outcry against the cane, that masters have been driven to the extreme and don't *now* resort to it enough.

But we must of course know that most of these matters, as the cane, roll-call, hours for games, etc., are beyond our province, still on the point of *hours for lessons* we can urge that boys should not be pressed in the early morning on an empty stomach, nor directly after their mid-day dinner, for that surely is a time when the blood can be better employed in the work of digestion than being forced to the brain, thus weakening the digestion *and* brain power of every lad who tries to do his duty.

We can also represent the often overlooked fact that the lower school cannot work at lessons as many hours in a day as the upper school. A boy of eleven not so long surely as a boy of eighteen without damaging his health, if his brain is actually working during the time assigned for lessons.

But the difficulty will arise how is spare time to be employed if hours of work are decreased. And I can only trust you will some of you be able to gather a few hints to take back to your respective schools, after you have heard all I want to say on the management of athletics and the hours of recreation.

A great deal has lately been shown by those who have compared at board schools the work of half timers, contrasting so favourably with that of whole timers, and Charles Kingsley (than whom I cannot quote a finer authority on such a question) says, " the certain physical law that in order to renovate the brain day by day, the growing creature must have plenty of fresh air and play, and that the child who learns for four hours and plays for four hours, will learn more, and learn it more easily, than the child who learns for the whole eight hours."

But the centre and mainspring of physical education in public schools must continue to be those great games, the organised growth of centuries, which not only supply to most the prime necessities of exercise and recreation, but promote many desirable qualities of character. And if they are put on their right footing and cordially recognised as co-ordinate in the school system it will be easy then to prevent any contest between work and games.

And of games I must place first cricket and football, then gymnastics, drilling, swimming, running, rowing, skating, racquets, and fives.

Before going into each branch of athletics separately, let me try and show you how games may be so managed as to fulfil all the purposes of a *sound* physical education simultaneously with a good intellectual development.

Games supply that active EXERCISE, which I contend is as important a factor of vigorous health as proper drainage, pure water or fresh air.

These games supply RECREATION neither unwholesome nor demoralising. But remember some recreations do not supply much EXERCISE, and remember that *formal exercise,* whether the mile measured walk or in shape of the machine-like work of gymnastics do not supply *recreation.*

A large number of boys at our schools do not get any exercise at all, or at any rate, not nearly enough. A few occupy too much time at cricket and become too tired for school work, while those who need exercise the most, get it the least. Such as those who have been indulged at home, coddled and muffled up and on the fair way to grow up feeble men, loafing round the pastry cooks, indulging in luxuries, and who are inclined to underwork their bodies, from a naturally lethargic temperament, the lazy fellow, the loafer; and if you do not compel such an one to enter into games, you are doing wrong. When they grow bigger lads they will play only when they are compelled, preferring a novel over the fireside. Perchance they may cook up enough interest in sports to watch the victories or defeats of their school or house, and may even become worshippers at a distance of athletic prowess, which they can never hope to emulate, and the really good element in which, they are not trained to see.

Another class of boys who need compulsory athletics, and seldom get them, are the book prodigies. Boys who are inclined to overwork their brains to the neglect of their bodies, either because their brains are specially active or because they are stimulated by ambition to overwork them.

Clever young boys by judicious forcing bear fruit early, and gain an entrance scholarship at a good school. Perhaps they hold further on with their forcing and go up to Oxford or Cambridge with an open scholarship, and later on obtain a good degree. These boys if predisposed naturally to be somewhat feeble in bodily constitution, become more and more unfitted for the struggles and duties of every day life. Now, if they had been early taught, that scholastic success is not incompatible with physical training, what much more vigorous healthy men they would have made; and so let us try and eradicate from schools these two classes of boys, the self-indulgent lounger and the pale narrow-chested prematurely forced book-worm.

I am sure many a small boy preparing for entrance scholarships at Preparatory Schools is injuriously affected by premature and excessive brain excitement at an early age, which lowers the vitality and vigour of body and mind.

You will agree with me that no schools require the hours of recreation to be so carefully looked after as the Preparatory Schools, for the seeds of the future Public School-boy are sown there and must be done with a careful judicious hand.

Out of the various Athletic exercises I above enumerated,

each might require pages to be written upon it, but I hope to dispense with several in a few words, and although I do not lose sight of the vast importance of swimming yet I am inclined to place first of all Drilling.

Drilling.—In every school let us hope each boy is drilled from the smallest to the biggest; and the first point is that he shall be *bodily* fit for the amount of drill imposed upon him; then that there shall be a good Drill Instructor, not of an irritable hasty temper, but a firm honest man who not only understands his drill but also knows how to teach it.

With the exception of the Gymnasium, the boy is more dependent upon his *teacher* in drill than in any other athletic exercise. The medical officer will pass most boys as fit and the delicate boy as fit for only a certain amount of drill. Let the doctor keep a special eye that the delicate boy is not over-drilled, and though it scarcely is within our province, yet it cannot hurt us to know the drill instructor does not needlessly bully or worry a timid lad who often does not understand a tenth of what is being said to him. The hours of drill should not be too long and they should not be on an empty stomach.

And as far as you can help it, do not let the drill be mere mechanical drudgery, got through somehow or other by the lad who is anxious to be off elsewhere. Never allow "punishment drill" but try and push forward the claims of the Rifle Corps quite as part of the School System, that in the Upper School every boy shall be a member of it and in the Lower School a member of the Cadet Corps, both of these carrying out the more advanced stages of the simple drill of the smallest boy entering a school.

From 120 schools written to, I have collected the following facts about Rifle Corps and Drilling.

A Rifle Corps in 13 per cent.

Drilling in some form or other in 82 per cent.

No Rifle Corps, no Drilling at all in 18 per cent.

And I will here remark in passing that when I commenced this paper, I determined not to weary you with too many figures and statistics, but the form of paper passed round* is a copy of what I sent to the Medical Officer or Headmaster of 130 Schools and I have the results of nearly 100 replies. I will not give you in a mass, pile upon pile of percentages, but I will give you separately the result of my enquiries upon each branch, and at the end a summary of the answers received on general matters.

Next to Drilling I think Swimming must be taken, and here we shall have I hope parents, headmasters, and doctors all agreeing that every boy shall learn to swim— of course the quantity and quality of his swimming will vary with each boy. But when we agree that each boy shall be compelled to swim, I might perhaps add 20 yards as a minimum. If he chooses to do more by all means let him, but surely it is not too much to require that a boy should swim that distance. Here as in the question of drill, both doctor and instructor must bear an important point.

It would be hard to persuade me that bathing will hurt a lad and I shall assume the medical officer passes the boy as fit for bathing. I must own it is rather a disgrace to the past generation of this country, that to be able to swim is an attainment possessed by so few. Let us strenuously *urge* upon parents and headmasters that every boy shall be compelled to learn to swim.

During four years of my residence at Cambridge there were several deaths from drowning amongst men I knew, caused not by cramp but by inability to swim, and at last a law has been passed that *no* undergraduate shall take a boat up the river who cannot sign his name in a book kept in the boathouse, as able to swim. A step decidedly wanted, but let us hope that in the present rising generation all will learn to swim—both boys and girls—and we can safely promise that no one will ever repent it, for not only are we here teaching a boy a pleasant healthy exercise, but also how to save his own life and the lives perhaps of others. With swimming we naturally associate bathing and we must be firm in not allowing boys to bathe too often in one day nor for too long a time. The plan of running about naked and getting in and out of the water a score of times during an hour,

* *Vide* Appendix A.

is a very bad habit, and the presence of the swimming master is most essential, and in the case of small boys the presence of an under-master is most desirable to prevent any bullying and ducking the timid lad.

At Highgate having no river near, there is a large swimming bath attached to the school where the water is kept slightly warmed, and so far we have never heard of any ill results from every boy bathing.

The hot water enters at the bottom of the shallow end and the cold leaves at the surface in the deep end, the Temperature being generally 65° F.

The results from the 100 schools I find to be most interesting, and it is curious to see how much more unanimous they all are on the point of swimming compared to any other branch of athletics; 91 per cent. have provisions for boys learning to swim, but only 18 per cent. compel every boy to learn, and some of these *compel* only because of the boating attached to the school.

From swimming, on which I fear I have dwelt at some length, I pass next to the GYMNASIUM, and here we pre-suppose the same facts that we did about drilling, namely, that each boy is passed by the Medical Officer as healthy, and fit for work in the gymnasium. A few delicate boys being allowed only to do the simpler and lighter work according to their bodily fitness and capabilities.

Every boy ought to have regular instruction in gymnastics. It has been proved that the average chest girth of boys from 14 to 19 years of age should be greater than it usually is. This has been clearly shewn in a pamphlet, which has been sent me for perusal, by the Head-master of a large school where physical education has been more than usually systematized*, (and whose boys have shewn marked proficiency in athletics, football, cricket, &c., at Oxford), and it is obvious that a raised average of chest girth throughout the country would imply increased vigour of constitution, and decreased liability to many diseases.

Gymnastics are a most excellent form of exercise, especi-

* For a summary of measurable results so far as chest-girth is concerned, and the points of the system which seem to have a bearing on these results *vide* Appendix B.

ally in correcting the tendency to round shoulders, stooping habits, slouching gait, and increasing the chest girth, but do not let us substitute either gymnastics or drilling for *play* and *recreation*, and athletics in that sense of the word. Remember, we are not imposing tasks upon the boy.

The muscular formal movements, the machine-like work of drill, excellent in their way, lack the variety and interest found in our games, they sooner induce fatigue, as there is the lack of COMPETITION and excitement that we find in cricket, fives and other games. But there is no doubt that by a well-devised system of gymnastics the most thorough exercise of every set of muscles in the body may be secured, and such education of the muscles will imply not only increase of actual strength but greater rapidity and versatility of action, more adroitness and precision of movement, more skill in the combination of forces; and the right use of that skill will make all the difference to a boy's success in games whatever branch of athletics he may take up.

So where a gymnasium is found in our Schools, let us encourage gymnastics, and let them be systematically undertaken under a paid competent instructor. If boys are turned loose into a gymnasium, they will probably do themselves more harm than good. The exercises should be designed for the requirements of each, and should be steadily increased, and a record might be kept of its effect on their physique.

But do not let all this *take the place* of other branches of athletics, more especially as it has rather a tendency to develop the upper limbs chiefly. Let us encourage it (and drilling) as a *necessary part* of the EDUCATION.

60 per cent. I find have a gymnasium; only 45 per cent. a paid teacher, and only 10 per cent. a record kept.

In leaving these three branches, drilling, swimming, gymnastics, I pass to what I might call a separate group, inasmuch as these three require an instructor, I might say a paid competent instructor, without whom boys cannot learn the simple rudiments, still less hope to make any progress.

Of our next group, I am inclined to place first for our notice ATHLETIC SPORTS, running, jumping, weight-putting, hurdle racing. Here I may tell you I am thoroughly at home, when I offer you any remarks, from having been President of my College Athletic Club three years, and having competed in many races, and been judge in athletic sports down to the present time.

Now these athletic sports are of no use, if they are to be the speciality of a few who are stared at by the rest, and who compete for prizes of preposterous value, but they are an unmixed blessing if every boy joins in them. Although not often carried out, I can bear witness to the popularity of the system where every boy has his performances registered at weekly intervals and their athletics occupy odd days throughout the whole spring, with prize competitions at the end.

Let us encourage every healthy lad to run—he can soon find out for himself whether he can ever excel at it—he will find out whether *pace* for short distances or strength of wind is his strong point in running—he will not excel in *long* AND *short* distances. When he has found out his strong point, if it is pace, tell him on authority of some of our best sprint-runners, that in addition to pace, two things are required for success; a good start, and a bright cheerful confident feeling at the time of the Race. I have seen one of the finest sprint-runners a short time before his 100 yards race slightly out of sorts, either from an undigested breakfast or from a fit of the blues, and beaten by men to whom he could give a few yards on the days when he felt bright and cheerful.

If the boy turns out to be a long distance runner, encourage him to go in for paper chases. And tell any boys when practising never to half run at their given distances, but always to run as if in a race, and above all things encourage the spirit and pluck in a boy. Watch a race at your school to see character and temper, a boy without pluck will not do his utmost if pressed, but shows the white-feather quickly, and a boy with pluck and determination, though not so good a runner, presses him more and more and finally beats him, if not in that race he does in the next, or in the world's race for life.

Let us not think little of running, for in the Zulu war an old Oxford mile runner, ran with the colours and saved them, as well as his life and many others in his regiment.

It is not within the province of my paper to write an essay on *training;* this can be obtained from many books—too many I fear. But still as Medical Officers to the schools, we shall be enabled to help the growing boy with sound advice as to *simple general laws of health,* and the due regard to these constitutes the foundation of real training.

If we teach boys to apply the elements of practical physiology to every day-life, they will learn the value of fresh air in their school rooms, and dormitories at night, they will learn something about digestion, why the stomach requires rest after food, and many such things.

There would not be that sudden change of diet and hours now too common in going *in* and *out* of training; in short *bodily* training like *mental,* ought to be a normal and CONSTANT condition, rather than an EXCEPTIONAL. Violent and sudden changes or strains either for examinations or for athletics are in themselves injurious. And just as *mental culture not* examinations ought to be the chief end of *intellectual* education, so a *condition of body* not only free from disease, but full of vigour and high spirits ought to be the goal of a *rational physical* training.

Training should be gentle regular *systematic* exercise, with sound wholesome diet, not that old-fashioned rigid dietary of half-cooked animal flesh, which is a descendant of the empirical methods of our prize-fighters—not that exhaustive physical work which some professionals still insist upon.

The old-fashioned idea of running before breakfast till you are fit to drop, of having one's food and drink weighed and measured, and being compelled to eat *nolens volens,* and to be purged periodically whether requisite or not, all this has disappeared with the advent of more sensible views of health. For each boy to go through the *same* training is manifestly absurd. The overfed fat boy requires reducing; the thin wiry lad requires feeding and keeping in form; the lazy lie-in-bed must be got up early, and all must be made to go to bed early to get the best of the night for their first sleep.

Let us not think their athletics beneath our observation, let us as far as possible help each boy in his training, and encourage him to persevere, if at any time watching them practising rowing, fives, racing or any other sport, tell them to do every detail most thoroughly, not to waste their strength and energies in slovenly practise and in acquiring bad habits, and remember, a word of encouragement or *advice* from one standing in the position we occupy, is of priceless value to the lad entering into manhood. I have found it a capital plan, to let every boy feel and know that he can come to the doctor as a *friend* at any time for counsel and advice in all matters, connected with health and training, and depend upon it such advice given at an early age will not be thrown away.

When discussing training with a boy, let us mention that SMOKING is strictly forbidden, and for *men* in strict training it is very bad. No harm can be done by this for we shall all agree that smoking for boys at school is certainly not to be advocated. If it is indulged in, it must be on the sly; it must be away from the boy's study and play-ground, away from his companions, and it develops therefore by its necessary act of disobedience, a tendency towards a boy slinking away either by himself or with one or two more at the most, and it is encouraging meanness and deception in his disposition leaving alone the effect on his health, which of course is open to a wide difference of opinion.

On such questions as drinking, late hours, etc., I think we need scarcely touch, if we remember we are dealing with boys. But we can show them, that for training a great deal must be left to a boy's honour. This will open a boy's eyes (perhaps for the first time) to the fact of keeping his body in subjection—and of course we get a chance of putting a drag on the well-greased wheel of the pastry cooks and confectioners, and let us do that only with caution and judgment. I do not believe cakes, tarts, or ginger beer, *et hoc genus omne* in anything like moderation, will hurt a boy, but what I do object to, is the hanging about the shop for two or three hours at a stretch learning the early stages of gossip and loafing.

Before leaving the subject of *training*, there is one more point I will allude to, and that is the table beer offered to the boys. Do not misunderstand me that one glass of good ale will hurt a growing lad with his dinner—not at all—but let me emphasize, ONE glass and GOOD ale. The beer at most schools is not what we should like to drink, and to a thirsty boy it will not do any good.

Water is all that is required and for my part, I always urge it upon the healthy lad at school.

I have lately remarked, and that too with pleasure, the large number of boys who always drink water. Out of the last dozen boys from our largest public school I have met with, eleven drank water at midday meals, and over 30 per cent. were drinking water at my old college table in Cambridge last year compared to 4 per cent. nineteen years ago.

I fear I have left the question of races somewhat too long, but I felt bound to express a few points on *training* as I consider it affects the boys.

To return to the question of running, some of you will be surprised to hear that the long distances are not the races which do most harm to a boy or man. A paper-chase is often one of the happiest afternoons which a lad can pass. He gets over some ten or a dozen miles, he has a variety of cross country to get over, and gets into places he would never see at any other time, very little plain running, plenty of variety and excitement all the time, and, you may not believe it, plenty of walking—remember a boy's paper chase is not like the cross country races now so prevalent in the distant suburbs of London along country roads, where the whole course is known beforehand.

And the boy out of training and with a bad wind soon finds himself left so far behind, he makes for home. The tough few persevere, and all who can should be encouraged to run to the end.

The mile race in athletics is virtually open only to those the Head Master or Medical Officer think fit to allow to start. But the *hard* and if I may so call, the DANGEROUS race is the quarter mile; this is granted by all athletes, and let me urge you if *any* question of weak health arises in a boy, *forbid* him to run the quarter.

The 100 yards is a quick burst from beginning to end, and whilst it is being run you do not take a breath, as it is finished under eleven seconds, but the quarter is started at the same burst, your top speed which has to be maintained all along, with a terrible strain at the end for a *spurt.* There is no time to slacken and ease off as in the mile, and the last fifty yards are forced out without any previous rest as in the longer races.

If I seem to you to enter to fully on these various matters of detail, let me assure you I do so on good grounds, and if I call your attention to forbidding the quarter rather than the mile in question of doubt, I shall not have written in vain.

I may mention one of the surgeons to St. George's Hospital, Morgan of Trinity College, Oxford, won the three mile race against Cambridge for three successive years, yet he could never have attempted the quarter, and to watch him run, you could feel confident he was able to go on for a day or two at that pace without injuring himself, differing from another Oxford man, Wilson of Worcester College, who won the 100 yards for three successive years about the same time, and once was persuaded to try the quarter, but fell from sheer exhaustion in the last 50 yards.

We will leave now the question of running, by saying, encourage it all you can in the healthy lad, especially the happy days of an honest paper-chase—encourage *simple* training, and when in doubt forbid the quarter.

With the question of jumping, both the high jump, long, and pole, we can have very little to say. If a boy can jump let him; and if he breaks a limb do NOT let us discourage others as that is an accident pure and simple which might happen from any cause.

But *putting the weight* and *hammer throwing* are branches of athletics with which I have very little sympathy for GROWING boys, severe strains on the body are suddenly given, and though the weight-putting may develop the muscles of the thorax and arm, yet I believe more harm than good is caused by both of these.

From athletic sports I pass to the finest of all games in the civilized world, that of *cricket*, and here I must introduce a few words about FAGGING, as in many schools it is associated with time-honoured customs in relation to cricket.

During the past twenty years GREAT changes have taken place in our schools, and perhaps no changes more marked than in the corporal punishment by masters, and in the fagging by bigger boys. Whilst we all recognize the fact that the changes are in an onward and progressive direction, both for the comfort, peace and health of the boys, let us take care that we do not fall into the opposite extreme, and find that our boys are growing up in too much comfort and luxury.

To those of you who have been at public schools, the terms *fagging* and *bullying* have no points of resemblance, but the anxious parent, I fear, would think you an inhuman monster if you expressed a hope, that her son would be well fagged at school. The BULLY of a school is generally a middle-sized lad, too big or too old himself to be a fag, and not high enough in the school to be allowed fags of his own. If a small boy gets under a good big fellow as his fag, he will protect him from the bully, he will see to the small boy's interest, and the lad is happier than if left alone.

So with cricket—I am of opinion that every small boy who is fit for a public school should be *compelled* to play cricket, as a small boy let him fag at the nets to one of the eleven for a certain time every day, say half-an-hour, and let him also have his own cricket with his equals. There will thus, at any rate, be some means of shortening the time which is loafed away by many boys, and as long as the fagging is not too severe, and left in safe honest hands of the eleven, or those of similar standing in the school, we need have very little to fear.

At present in most schools the elevens practice with assiduity, the competitors for places in the elevens usually with mischievous excess frequently prejudicial both to themselves and their cricket. Good cricketers will tell you that the habit of trusting to a professional bowler for practice is not only prejudicial to the school bowling, but has a bad effect upon the elevens. They do not get enough practice at bowling, and they do not pick out stray unnoticed boys, who only require the chance and judicious teaching to become useful bowlers. Moreover, it is encouraging habits of indolence to have a professional bowling away by the hour.

Let a certain time daily be compulsory during the summer months, for every boy to be compelled to play cricket in the lower school. Those boys who are not playing in any house match or pick-up sides, let them be compelled to play at the nets, to field or long stop for the bigger boys. You will soon see the boy shows taste for the game, some hidden talent either as a long-stop or cover point or even wicket-keeper, and on the principle of the survival of the fittest, by the time he reaches the upper school he will be a cricketer, or show so little talent for the game that he may give it up: but we have the satisfaction of knowing that he had every opportunity for becoming a player. These remarks about fagging at cricket, apply but with much less force to *football* also. During the winter months a certain amount of compulsory exercise is most desirable, and football undoubtedly has the greatest hold on our schools at the present moment. Let every boy be compelled to play for a short time on half-holidays.

Let the matches for small-boys be arranged only amongst themselves. No heavy eleven stone lad charging a little fellow six stone, but boys of the same size should play together in the lower school.

Football undoubtedly develops qualities which are in the highest degree useful in life—courage, coolness, unselfishness, and presence of mind.

The danger of accidents at football I know is greater than all other games put together, but if it gives some work to the surgeon, it takes some away from the physician; and one of my great reasons for advocating it is that there are not those expensive surroundings, nor those luxurious lunches,

2

nor absorb crowds applauding gallery strokes, nor inordinate demands upon pocket and time.

The game of Football is such a national game now, that whether we approve or disapprove of it, we must endeavour to minimize its evils as much as possible, and here I can offer you a caution, and it is founded on experience of my own and from the experience of many others, both football players and doctors. This is the game of all others which requires the best heart and lungs. To play this game at all a boy must have lungs and heart in first rate order. I have had many University players tell me, a long day's cricket even with a good innings and bowling for one's side, does not try the *strength* so much as an hour and a half (the recognised time) football.

You will see this by the fact of our great cricketers playing every day, for six months, in matches. But no football player plays more than twice a week, and then only for a sixth of the time in the day.

The roughness, the temper, the brutality, and those points of the individual boy, belong to the Head-master not to the Medical Officer.

So I may conclude my remarks about Football by saying, every boy *ought* to play who is fit for it, and though some who have been delicately brought up do not like it at first, almost every boy with any spirit in him likes it in the end.

But some boys are *not* fit, and these should be the special care of any house-master who knows his work. If something else is not found for them to do, they get into loafing habits, and not only in the future grow up into feeble men, but I have found such lads more prone to take infectious disorders, and thus are another source of anxiety in a school.

It should be remembered that as regards COMPULSION in games, BODILY exercise should be as carefully supervised by the masters as MENTAL exercise; for it is not wise that boys should be left to manage these physical matters entirely by themselves, thinking that you can trust nature and all will come right, and that the boy for whom exercise is desirable, will be prompted by nature to take just the amount required for his health. No such thing. In the general routine of lessons a boy is compelled to conform to certain rules for the education of his mind, this is not here left to nature nor to the boy's disposition, for if it were there would, in most instances, be a miserable deficiency of brain exercise, or in a few rare cases a mischievous excess. If a boy does not like his Virgil or his Euclid, his masters do not leave him to take what he likes of those subjects, he is compelled to enter into them and to get through a certain amount, and often will soon excel in some branch of study from judicious compulsion. So with games, do not allow the boy to play only when he chooses; at any rate you are improving his bodily vigour and he has had every chance of excelling in some branch of Athletics. Let it be fairly instilled into minds of parents and masters that the education of the *Body* is not far behind the education of the *Mind* in importance, and the *amount* and *kind* of exercise both of mind and body should be always considered together.

From Cricket and Football I pass on to Fives and Racquets. It is not every School that possesses good Racquet and Fives Courts. Where a Fives court is found let me beg of you to encourage the game with all your power, for it is the grandest OUTDOOR game you will meet with. No revengeful feeling can be brought into play as in Football. Remember this is chiefly a winter game, and it is during the winter months we meet with the greatest difficulty in providing occupation and amusements, as it were in the interregnum between Cricket and Football.

We must bear in mind that in advocating games as an employment, for the spare time of boys, they must not necessarily think that their time is to be filled up *for them*, and occupation PROVIDED for every hour in either lessons or games. Let the boys learn to find some method by which they may best fill the spare time up for themselves, for if the boys who generally have their play hours fully occupied, are left without any definite attractive game, the harm is great, not only to their physical training but also to the tone of the school, and I am not acquainted with any game where so much exercise, of the most healthy kind, is met with as in Fives and Racquets, and it is exercise of the most desirable nature for it develops the muscles of the upper and lower limbs equally. It necessitates remarkable agility and quickness of movement, a keen eye, and precision in striking.

There is no standing still as in cricket, no fear of heavy charges and damaged limbs as in football. In short this game stands out alone, in my opinion, for splendid exercise.

I knew several hard reading men at Cambridge, who could not find time during the last few weeks before an examination, for a common amount of exercise, who always said they could get as much good out of an hour's Racquets or Fives as out of three or four hours Cricket or Boating in the general way.

We must, however, remember that a good and perfect Racquet court is only met with at the very best Schools, and as Racquets is somewhat an expensive game it can only be played by a few of the bigger boys. But between Fives and real Racquets there are several stages, and such games as Bat Fives, Out-door Racquets, Soft Ball Racquets, are more to be encouraged than any other games in the whole list. If any of you have ever played Bat Fives or Racquets out-of-doors with two side walls and a soft ball, you will agree with me that here you reach all that is desired for a boy's exercise and amusement. It can be played on an uncovered court by all sizes and at as little cost as cricket.*

If once you can impress the Headmasters or the Governors of the School with the value of Fives, it is astonishing how soon odd corners against walls and buildings in the playground can be utilized and turned into a Bat Fives' Court. Never mind the exact size, anything in length from 20 to 40 feet and in breadth half that will suffice, and no parents nor boys will ever lament the introduction of Fives and Racquets in any shape to the school.

* Of the Schools I enquired from 75 per cent. have Fives Courts of some sort or another.

There are a few so called sports which, though splendid in themselves, are open to many objections at schools, and I must allude to them before ending my list of various Athletic exercises.

Boxing and Fencing are branches which should be learnt, but they should come within the province of the Gymnasium and certainly must be *taught* PROPERLY to be of any use. They should not be allowed anywhere except IN the Gymnasium and under the eyes of the proper Instructor, and not to boys under twelve years of age. Do not allow boxing gloves, foils or singlesticks in the studies or school-rooms on any account. They are a means of *bullying*, and they may be said to encourage it if allowed indiscriminately amongst the boys by themselves. Many a boy is made to box and fence simply as a means of bullying him, and all courage gets knocked out of a small boy if he knows he is put to *box* with a nasty tempered lad, and only two or three jeering companions looking on, and nobody to see fair play.

In schools where boxing is allowed, take great care the gloves are never allowed to be taken into a school-room or a boy's study, as they can do no good with them there, and singlesticks and fencing foils should all be carefully locked up and only allowed to be used under the eye of the Instructor or one of the masters.

There is one branch of Athletic exercise I cannot pass over, and yet very little can be said upon it, I allude to Skating; taking an average we can only count upon finding strong ice one year in four, and when it does come it is nearly always in the holidays and so outside our notice as Medical Officers to Public Schools.

But from finding only 13 per cent. of large schools that boys are compelled to learn swimming, let us ask the Headmaster to forbid any boy on ice till he can swim, exactly as they forbid in 74 per cent. any boys to ROW. It will be another way of attaining a good object, that every boy SHALL learn to swim.

Let us also persuade the very smallest boy to skate and to do it well. Now is the time to learn figure skating. If not learnt during youth you will never learn it, for a tumble or heavy fall in later years is attended with very different results to the same falls in youth, then moreover it is the natural instinct fearing to fall which prevents an older man from trying the many figures. For exercise on a clear frosty day nothing can come near it, and we can leave this with one remark, encourage it in every possible way, without any hesitation or reserve, to the very smallest boy.

I think now I have gone seriatim over each branch of athletic games, as generally met with in any schools, I have dwelt perhaps at too great a length on some branches, but I trust I have given you clearly my views on them.

I think the tone of schools has somewhat altered since "Tom Brown" was written in respect to bird's nesting, butterfly catching, etc. These and other kindred pursuits are more to be met with in books and in a past generation, than in the modern school-boy with whom we have to deal, and besides this I do not think the insect hunting boy quite comes within the scope of my paper.

I must make a few remarks which will apply to all games I have mentioned, as regards the boy from a physical point of view.

We will assume that every boy should be seen by the Medical Officer soon after he enters the school, and that a medical report of him is sent from home.

We must endeavour to see that each boy's constitution is robust and healthy and kept so, in as far as this can ever depend upon any school arrangements which are under our control. Let us ask the masters to receive our help in doing away with any legalised bodily idleness, and we shall soon see the physical languor and flabbiness disappear from the loafers and many a boy will improve visibly, bodily and mentally.

If a boy is found to be suffering from some constitutional disease or is decidedly delicate, we can put him at once out of the question of athletics. But some few boys may be *delicate* without being placed in *that* group, and for them a certain amount of exercise is beneficial. Let the Medical

Officer order the exercise and the branch of sport he thinks the boy is fit for and the amount of it. And now, if I may add the remark, let him see that he gets it; not necessarily see with his own eyes but through other trustworthy eyes, for frequently the *slightly* delicate boy trades on his weakness and does not really get the amount of exercise he should, or that would be good for him. The rough games, as football, I would of course prevent a lad from playing who is ruptured, and a boy with an ill-shaped pigeon-breasted chest I would forbid the quarter or the mile race.

But for all boys who are found to be healthy and up to the average, I would insist upon their entering into some sport or another. While insisting on all boys taking exercise, let us not forget that these health pursuits are of course limited in their action for good and may exist with every kind of moral disease, but the attainment of high morality without favourable physical surroundings and arrangements, is rendered much more difficult. And as an upright moral boy cannot always be *made*, let us do our best by advocating all favourable steps towards that end, remembering to enforce on the parents that there is no necessary antagonism between right physical development and right intellectual development, nor between robustness and refinement, nor bodily strength and mental culture. Either of these parts may be monstrously developed or neglected, but the simultaneous growth of both is what we desire. Do not let the boys learn to think lightly of a cultivated intellect because they only see it in weakly and neglected bodies, and thus get the idea, that to become successful in their studies they must neglect their constitution and strength, for the healthy athlete may be refined or unrefined, cultivated or uncultivated, and the culture gained at the expense of robust health we should always suspect, for it is from health not from disease, from strength not from weakness, that true culture and refinement emanate. Robust health is not to be sought after as an end in itself, but rather in the possession of that, all other undertakings can be more successfully carried out.

Do not let a boy deprive himself of his outdoor exercise; school is the place, boyhood is the time for the formation of all good habits; and regular daily exercise with some interest is a very valuable habit, and one hard to acquire later in life.

The bane of every school is the idle boy, idle as regards games as well as lessons. The boy who *won't* play. He is a constant worry to his master, being never out of mischief, a source of misery to himself, and very often a bully, having nothing better to do. Until parents see this we shall be ever having the constant outcry against COMPULSORY GAMES. Whereas IT IS THIS rule of compulsion which is one of the chief sources of a healthy tone in public schools.

Help boys to be manly, energetic and enthusiastic at their games, and you help them to be healthy and honest lads throughout their whole school life. Fail in this and you will have an unmanly precocity in self-indulgence; loafing and smoking boys becoming premature "men" of the world.

There is no doubt the worst boys intellectually, physically and morally are the *loafers*; the boys who work hard and play hard, do not ape the vices of men, and are free from the insidious evils that often fasten on UNOCCUPIED boyhood.

Therefore do away with the loafer, send him out, away from unhealthy emasculating demoralizing idleness to invigorating healthy exercise, and if you have any doubt about any boy who is healthy taking his part in games, call the attention of one of the masters or a prefect to him, and do not let a boy satisfy you that for exercise he *takes a walk*.

First of all a walk WITHOUT ANY OBJECT is scarcely healthy exercise. There is no competition in it, no honest rivalry, no occasion to put forth any energy or any skill and the brain gets no change from the tedium of the day.

Generally the "*walkers*," both men and boys, are to be avoided, that is to say, those who go out for a walk pure and simple without any aim or object, probably talking SHOP all the way, up to a given milestone and back again. He must have an unhealthy mind who can be satisfied with that for his exercise, and in boys at school, let us almost forbid it :—a couple of healthy boys sneak out for a walk by themselves day after day, leaving the cricket ground, the gymnasium, and the fives court, till those places know their faces no more. In the majority of boys out for a walk we may depend upon it, filthy talk and speculation upon the unknown laws of nature soon crop up in the smaller lads, followed by beastly books and loathsome actions in the bigger boys. They will get hold of a translation of forbidden pieces of Juvenal or Ovid, or of obscene pictures and gloat over them, and now they can get for a penny the *Pall Mall* as published last August, beyond that they will want no more.

Here, gentlemen, let me pause to make a passing remark, with which I shall have your fullest sympathy. Let the motives of those who undertook the Secret Commission of Modern Babylon be what they may, no filthy book ever found surreptitiously concealed by a small boy and procured at much trouble and cost, could come up to the undisguised bawd and filth scattered broadcast throughout England at a penny a copy, as we saw last summer in the *Pall Mall*. There was no occasion for boys to discuss the *unknown* any longer; here for a penny they had their fill, here they had details of every description graphically revealed to them which would be only defiling the ears of my audience if I were to enumerate. In one school I am told fourteen copies were found on that first Monday evening.

But passing back from that unsavoury topic, if we find a big boy of 17 or 18 walking out to a certain village for his exercise let us remember to enquire carefully into the public houses there and the morality of the young women about that place. No gentlemen, I cannot believe in a walker as a walker pure and simple.

But do not misunderstand me that I do not like walking, far from it—walking tours, and a good healthy occasional walk to a neighbouring town, all walks with *an object* are very different from what I am decrying. I may add that I have myself walked five times direct from Cambridge to London and twice accomplished the fifty-two miles in a night of fifteen hours.

And now leaving the question of *walking as an exercise,*

when we have decided such and such boys are fit for any games, let us insist on common sense rules. Let them dress for their games in suitable clothes, and there is nothing like white flannel for an all round general material for shirts, trousers and jackets.

Let the trousers be easy and loose and not tight round the waist, but fastened below the crest of the ilium, and for most games thick socks are desirable.

The chest and throat should be kept free and open at all times, but especially during any games. We can urge flannel shirts being worn at all times, and for my part I like those made with collar attached as it leaves the throat more open.

The boots also are a matter of great importance for in no part of our clothing is greater absurdity shewn than in some of the narrow-pointed high-heeled boots. For a proper fitting boot the great toe must be kept in a straight line. The moment this toe is diverted, its leverage power which brings into exercise the muscles and tendons of the foot with the consequent development of the arch of the instep is hindered. There must be low heels or you will weaken the arch by raising its heelbone abutment above the level of the meta-tarsus abutment. The sole should be thick and at the same time as yielding as a tennis shoe or you lose the internal play which is provided by nature in the plantar ligament.

It is a good plan to insist upon the whole school changing into flannels every day for a certain time. A boy can play more easily in flannels at any game, and is more likely to join in a chance game if dressed suitably, for very few will care to hang about in flannels doing nothing, and we are more certain he will change after games, which is most necessary, especially after much exertion, and this should be carefully carried out as regards the undergarments, for often a boy will change his flannel trousers, neglecting his shirt and socks.

There should be a separate room for drying the damp clothes, which ought never to be left all night in their bed-rooms.

To some of you these details must appear dry and wearisome, and I fear I have tired you by taking you at such length through all the branches of athletics as I have done, and if I appear to be dry and egotistical my excuse must be my own love of athletics of all sorts, and the curious want of knowledge met with amongst the world in general on these familiar topics. Many people pooh-pooh fives as a feeble edition of racquets or look on all races as sure means for an early death. Another point of ignorance is the question of fagging, and here I must refer to fagging at cricket, encourage it all you can, and disabuse the ignorant mind that it is of necessity associated with the harsh treatment of their dear boy.

Perhaps to many I may appear an enthusiast riding too strongly a hobby horse—I hope not, for no one knows better than I do the opposite side to the view I have been endeavouring to place before you.

Believing as I do in the necessity of plenty of out-door *exercise*, I believe also in its control; and the EXCESS of it as well as its DEFICIENCY is very prejudicial to the welfare of the boy. Do not let the masters and parents suppose our great aim is that boys should necessarily have MORE exercise, but rather that they should have that amount and kind of exercise, which seems to be right for increasing bodily and mental vigour. Athletics like everything else can be sought after too much, and perhaps I shall be told at the present day they do occupy too prominent a position. If so, let us improve that position, let us strengthen the foundation and remove the dangers as far as in us lies.

If we could get masters and parents to realize the importance of combining a scientific AND intellectual training, what would become of the present system of competitive examination. At present in this country at a critical time of life when growth is most rapid, boys who aspire to high military, or Indian, or home civil service, appointments are not only over-strained mentally, but placed under most unfavourable physical conditions, as regards exercise at the various establishments of the crammers. I do not blame these gentlemen, *marks* pay and physique does not, so they devote their whole attention towards enabling their pupils to win marks, and the consequence is that we are selecting as civil servants, and even officers, many of inferior or damaged physique.

Let candidates for public appointments show that they have physical vigour, and that their *body* as well as their *mind* has received a good general education and development. They should show proficiency in most athletic exercises, but no encouragement should be given to physical feats, for on the same ground that we discourage mental forcing, so we must take care no sort of physical forcing is allowed. A certain standard to be reached is what should be aimed at.

I am not advocating by any means a system of choice by physical qualifications alone, but I do hope to see carried out much more fully, the system of both physical and intellectual qualifications scoring marks, as we see already in a few cases, as I believe for example in the Woods and Forest department of the civil service, where each candidate has to run different distances, to jump, to put the weight, etc., and in each branch of sport a minimum standard is fixed for every candidate to attain to.

This will show you that athletics have taken hold on the public mind of England, and if we can help them on in a healthy direction we are doing well. Let us see that all games are based upon healthy rules, and take care that a boy does not enter too vigorously for them to the exclusion of everything else, nor enter for the branches of sport for which he is physically unfit.

A boy who excels in out-door work, does not always shine in lessons, but as long as he is not allowed to over-work himself at games he is not taking away from the power and strength of mind and brain. At most schools games are superintended by the prefects, who are chosen from the upper part of the sixth form, not always a judicious plan, for a prefect should be chosen on the grounds of his force of character and proved worth, and boys would see that there are some places at school, as well as in the world, where cleverness *alone* gains neither honour nor power, but these are bestowed upon character and moral force. And it is constantly observed that the boy who has been made much of at school as an athlete seldom succeeds afterwards, partly because he has run himself out when too young, and overstrained his frame at a critical time of life. Let us try and instil a healthy form of game. Let us correct absurd ideas about training and hardships and fagging. Let us try and direct each boy we may come across in some branch of sport where he may excel, let us show him the pitfalls of each sport, and where mistakes are to be avoided and where expected.

Then let us look on athletics not only as a recreation for the body but for the mind also, as a means for the end. The end of getting a good place amongst your school-fellows or your college friends, and the great end of getting on in life. Books and studies at school are of course most necessary, else perhaps we should not send our boys there, and that we may help the masters to improve the mind, let the doctor do his best to keep a healthy active frame in the body.

I am sure for my part I should like to see a son excel in both mind and body, and I should not fret if he were to sink from a second to a third class, if by that neglect of study and book-lore he had gained a place in his University Eleven or Boat; but I am not implying that I should like him to grow up a dunce with his place in the eleven—far from it—but I should know what his body was going through and that for such a position he was at any rate practising self-denial in many ways, and I should feel proud to see him come home with his Blue Ribbon and Medal—for remember these are indeed heirlooms, which no money can purchase, no family blood give you a claim to, but only acquired by those who have successfully gone through the struggle and competition for them against the picked amateurs of England.

The day has not yet arrived when the public examinations of schools so ably conducted by the Universities, will embrace not only classics and mathematics and brain work, but also a physical examination of the whole school. I should like to see as a test of a school's greatness, that the boys are living under the strict laws of health and exercise and able to endure certain BODILY strains as well as MENTAL.

If the examinations were so conducted, every boy (with the exception of those abnormally constituted) would be expected to reach a certain qualifying standard of mental and physical proficiency combined, and must show in addition to a well developed brain, a robust and healthy mind in a strong and healthy body.

I know that no regulations about the employment of spare time can *make boys moral*, but if we force them to live healthy vigorous lives, we help them greatly towards honest moral lives.

And now in conclusion, what can we each individually do towards all this?

I can assure you that in the school of over 300 boys, all boarders, to which I was medical officer for several years, I seldom had a boy in the sick ward I could not make a friend of by entering into some branch of sport with him. I may flatter myself, but I think I made many friends amongst those boys solely by entering heart and soul into their games. They learnt in a moment I spoke with understanding and knowledge of my topic; they learnt in a moment that all the advice I gave them was sound and practical. They could respect my authority in matters of games and would appeal to me on numerous points for help; but I cannot expect you all to have my love for athletics nor to take the pleasure in them that I do, but beyond these points came that to which I will briefly draw your attention last, as it is one where I place my hopes that some good may follow the work expended on this paper.

You can tell them first the great consequence of having a pure body and a healthy frame, and how a pure mind will help to regulate this. You can show them how a boy, who indulges in any sexual evils and above all in self-abuse, is seriously handicapped in any branch of sport. You can tell them that all sins of lust are forbidden strictly to a man in training, and how important it is that for every game or match they shall train by keeping themselves from fleshly lusts. You may even go further with the bigger boys and show them that the debauched man cannot contest in any severe struggle, and that mentally and bodily he will be left the further behind in the struggle for existence.

They will listen to you I can assure you, and here you have a golden chance of helping to put down, the great evil of self-abuse, which we hear is so common in our schools. You will scarcely believe the oracle you the physician are to that boy. He sees you have no motive in helping him but his own bodily good. You are not paid to talk morality to him as he thinks his parish priest or his schoolmaster is, and if the doctor, as a friend, tells a boy these evils will ruin him and ruin at once his chances of success in games, you are indeed lending a helping hand towards putting down that evil. And that boy is a rare and strange creature who will not try and act upon advice given him, for no conceivable object but his own good, by a doctor who he sees is his friend, and if you watch his progress in games he will come to you frequently on those matters, and if he finds out for himself the difference in his vigour, you may depend upon it, your advice has done more good than all the sermons on morality ever preached.

I am not going to underrate the duties of parents and masters in showing a boy the rocks ahead. Let them do so. It is their bounden duty. But because a thing is *wrong* that will scarcely stop a boy from doing it. Show him it is *against his own interest*, against his chance of success, and you hit a more correct nail on the head.

And here let me call attention to two important books I have received during my enquiries on this matter, one from Dr. Dukes of Rugby and the other from Mr. Robertson the headmaster of Haileybury. They both encourage the *parent* telling their boy the evils of self-abuse and of fornication further on in life; they say it is wrong to allow the boy to set out in life in ignorance of these matters, and I cordially echo those sentiments; and my paper is to go a step in the same direction and even let the doctor help this matter on. Let the boy feel how much to his advantage it is, how much more he will shine in these games, how much better fitted for the contests of the playground as well as for the contest of life ; let him have his doctor's authority for it, that the fornicator and the onanist cannot stand the wear and tear of training and games, and many a lad for the sake of excelling in sports will leave these vices alone.

Gentlemen I have finished, and in concluding I must take this opportunity of thanking those headmasters and doctors who have replied so courteously to the circular I sent out, and I must thank you for your patient attention, to what I fear has been a somewhat rambling and unconnected paper, and if I can persuade any of you to take fresh interest in your boys and their athletics, I shall be satisfied, especially if I can instil my views into your minds (and they are views based upon a wide experience both of athletics and boys), and perchance we may through sports teach a boy the grand truth of self denial and of an honest and pure life, and if one boy is saved by your means from a weakened dissipated life, I shall feel that I have not written in vain.

Printed in accordance with a resolution passed at a General Meeting of the Medical Officers of Schools Association, on January 12th, 1886.

ALDER SMITH
CHARLES SHELLY } *Hon. Secs.*

APPENDIX A.—*Copy of circular sent to 130 Schools.*

1. Is there a Gymnasium in your School? Are the boys taught Gymnastics by a paid trained teacher?

Are the boys compelled to go through a course of Gymnastics?

Is any record kept of its effect on their Physique?

2. Is there a Swimming Bath? Is every boy *compelled* to learn Swimming? Is there a paid Swimming Master?

3. Is Cricket (or Football in Winter) compulsory for every small boy a certain time in the week? Either playing in a game amongst his own equals, or fagging for the bigger boys?

4. Is Drilling taught, either in a Rifle or Cadet Corps or in some other manner?

5. Have you a Racquet Court? Fives Court? Rifle Corps?

6. Have you a complete supervision over the Boys in training for any Athletic Sports?

7. Is adequate provision made for the boys to promptly change their wet flannels and jerseys after Athletics, Football, &c., and also for the drying of their flannels before they are used again?

8. Are all the boys *compelled* to enter into some game or other during the play hours in each week?

9. Can you offer me any suggestions with special reference to preventing boys loafing about and corrupting one another's morals?

APPENDIX B.   (Page 9).

The accompanying measurements of chest girth were taken three times a year by the same person, a sergeant-major who had been accustomed to take army measurements.

Every new boy's measurements are taken on arrival.

By "Old boys" is meant boys who have been at least three months at school.

OLD BOYS.

	Age 18.		Age 17.		Age 16.		Age 15.		Age 14.	
	No. of Boys.	Average in inches.	No. of Boys.	Average in inches.	No. of Boys.	Average in inches.	No. of Boys.	Average in inches.	No. of Boys.	Average in inches.
1877-83	87	36·8	209	35·1	286	34·3	334	32·5	256	31

NEW BOYS.

	Age 18.		Age 17.		Age 16.		Age 15.		Age 14.	
1874-83	2	32·5	8	33·2	17	32·2	35	30·6	53	29·3

The chief peculiarities in the system which has caused some of these results are :—

Firstly, every boy has half an hour's daily work in the gymnasium, which also is open to the boys at all times under an instructor's eye. Gymnastics, drill, sparring, etc., are in regular school hours, not deducted from playtime.

Secondly, every boy is also required to take a short run before breakfast, and at least half an hour's open air exercise (weather at all permitting) before dinner; and about an hour and a half between dinner and tea.

Thirdly, no impediments to the breathing organs in the shape of tight waistcoats and collars are allowed. In fact, waistcoats are seldom worn at all; the boys often wear flannel suits throughout the day—in cold weather a "sweater" is often worn instead of a waistcoat. And to the greater freedom in dressing are due some of the above improvements in chest girths.

THE END.

www.ingramcontent.com/pod-product-compliance
Lightning Source LLC
Chambersburg PA
CBHW081306040426
42452CB00014B/2676